Cornerstones of Freedom

The Story of
THE SALEM
WITCH TRIALS

By Zachary Kent

Illustrated by Ralph Canaday

 CHILDRENS PRESS ®

CHICAGO

Library of Congress Cataloging-in-Publication Data

Kent, Zachary.
  The story of the Salem witch trials.

  (Cornerstones of freedom)
  Summary: Discusses the social and religious conditions
surrounding the Salem witch hunts and describes the
ensuing trials and their aftermath.
  1. Trials (Witchcraft)—Massachusetts—Salem—Juven-
ile literature. [1. Witchcraft—Massachusetts—Salem.
2. Trials (Witchcraft)—Massachusetts—Salem]
I. Canaday, Ralph, ill. II. Title. III. Series.
KFM2478.8.W5K46 1986   345.744′50288   86-9632
ISBN 0-516-04704-3   347.44505288

Sheriff George Corwin led the five condemned women from Salem jail on the morning of July 19, 1692. Their chains rattled as the sheriff prodded them onto a cart. Farmers and townspeople jeered as they followed the cart over the rough road that twisted several miles southwest. From all over the Massachusetts countryside an excited mob collected on Gallows Hill to watch these witches hang.

The cart jolted to a stop at last, and the prisoners trudged up the rocky summit. As each stood upon a gallows ladder, Sheriff Corwin tied ropes around their necks. The Reverend Nicholas Noyes, Puritan minister of Salem, gave each woman a final chance to confess her crimes. Four of them quietly protested their innocence, but the fifth stood defiant. She was a dirty beggar woman named Sarah Good.

At her trial Sarah Good had been charged with riding a stick through the sky to attend witch meetings. Her husband claimed he had seen the devil's mark upon her body. Even her five-year-old daughter testified against her. The evidence condemning Sarah Good overwhelmed the Salem court.

Now the Reverend Mr. Noyes stepped before her. He knew she was a witch, he said, and he commanded that she admit it.

"You are a liar!" Sarah Good spit out. "I am no more a witch than you are a wizard, and if you take away my life God will give you blood to drink!"

A sudden hush swept over the crowd, while Noyes fell back in surprise. Surely only a witch could utter such a curse. Beneath the hot summer sun the hang-man received the deadly signal. The five women were pushed from their ladders. As their corpses dangled limply, the watching mob nodded, content that Salem was rid of five more witches.

These five were not the first to die, nor would they be the last. Throughout the year of 1692 a witchcraft scare seized the hearts and minds of everyone in Salem Village, a small farming community outside the town of Salem. "An Army of Devils is horribly broke in upon the place," wrote Boston minister Cotton Mather, "and the Houses of the Good People there are fill'd with the doleful shrieks of their Children and Servants." In the witch-hunt that followed, husbands suddenly suspected wives, and wives wondered about husbands. Neighbors pointed fingers, and hurried arrests brought the accused to trial. Minister John Hale later wrote that for a time "we walked in the clouds, and could not see our way."

English Puritans settled in Salem in 1630. Over the years the settlement endured disappointing harvests, hostile Indians, and rampaging diseases. The Puritans also lived with a burden of constant religious worries. From early childhood Puritans learned to fear death, destruction, and the devil. From his Boston pulpit, Cotton Mather warned that the Massachusetts forests had once belonged to the devil, and that the devil planned to conquer the Puritans and take his kingdom back.

This atmosphere of tension helped spark the witchcraft madness of 1692. In the early months of that year, during cold and idle afternoons, a group of girls gathered in the Reverend Samuel Parris's house in Salem Village. Around the kitchen fire they entertained themselves with scary stories of ghosts and spirits. With the help of Mr. Parris's slave, Tituba, they learned the forbidden art of fortune-telling by pouring an egg into a glass and reading its signs.

Then in February Mr. Parris's nine-year-old daughter, Betty, and his eleven-year-old niece, Abigail Williams, suddenly fell sick. The children's illness took the form of fainting fits, screams, and bizarre twistings of their arms and legs. Soon other girls, including twelve-year-old Anne Putnam, nineteen-year-old Mercy Lewis, and seventeen-year-old Elizabeth Hubbard, began acting in the same terrifying manner. In confusion, Dr. William Griggs revealed the only possible explanation.

"The evil hand is upon them," he announced.

Suddenly the neighborhood buzzed with talk of witchcraft. In that superstitious age the mere rumor of witches frightened most people. Some people used a charm, like a horseshoe nailed over the door, to keep these servants of the devil away. But when even prayers failed to stop them, it was believed witches gladly did the devil's bidding. Realizing this, the Reverend Mr. Parris lamented, "The devil hath been raised among us, and his rage is terrible."

In a rush to stem the crisis, Parris and others demanded to know who tormented the girls. The children offered the names of three local women: the kitchen slave Tituba, sickly old Sarah Osborne, and the beggar woman Sarah Good.

Anne Putnam's father quickly swore out a complaint against the three. On the morning of March 1 a great crowd packed the Salem Village meeting-house. The curious opened a path as the "afflicted girls" walked to seats near the front of the room. Two local judges arrived and ordered the start of the investigation. As Sarah Good was led into the room, the girls fell into a panic. Perhaps they enjoyed all the attention and excitement. Perhaps they were truly afraid. But they moaned and swayed, and rolled their eyes back in their heads.

"Their arms, necks and backs turned this way and that," recorded the Reverend Mr. Hale. "Sometimes they were taken dumb, their mouths stopped, their throats choked, their limbs wracked and tormented."

Judge John Hathorne (whose great-great-grandson, Nathaniel Hawthorne, would one day write famous stories about Salem) began the questioning.

"Sarah Good," he demanded, "have you made no contract with the devil? . . . Why do you hurt these children?"

"I do not hurt them. I scorn it," she answered nervously. The girls' behavior surprised her as much as it did the others in the meetinghouse.

"Who do you employ, then . . . what creature do you employ?" pressed Hathorne.

"No creature," the woman insisted. "I am falsely accused."

The judge then asked the children to look upon her. The speechless crowd watched as the girls twisted about and cried that she was the one who hurt them. They fell into the same shocking fits when Sarah Osborne entered the room. Greatly flustered, the old woman denied she had harmed the children. Only when the slave Tituba was brought forward did the people hear their first confession.

Scared out of her wits by the strange scene around her and led on by Judge Hathorne's questions, Tituba admitted she had "signed the devil's book" along with Good and Osborne. The devil came to her, she revealed, in the shapes of a black dog, a pig, and a rat, and promised her many fine things if she agreed to serve him. She claimed Sarah Osborne kept an ugly creature, "a thing all over hairy," to help her do evil tasks. It was three feet tall and walked like a man, "and last night it stood before the fire in Mr. Parris's hall."

The judges needed no further evidence. They immediately sent all three women to jail on suspicion of witchcraft.

These arrests did not stop the villagers' fears. In the weeks that followed, the troubled girls freely acted out their fantasies. In Mr. Parris's house, Abigail Williams one day hurled herself about and then made as if she would fly. Next she rushed to the fireplace, threw burning sticks about the room, and tried to climb up the chimney. In church she interrupted the solemn service with rude remarks. She pointed up to the rafters and claimed to see a witch there. "Look," she cried, "where Goodwife Corey sits on the beam!" Anne Putnam excitedly shouted that she also saw the woman. Within days Martha Corey found herself thrown in jail.

The nervous people of Salem Village asked themselves if more witches lurked about. They thought back and suddenly blamed sick children and sick farm animals, bad weather and bad luck all on the powers of witchcraft. Townsmen quickly remembered past arguments with farmers. Parents and masters suggested names and children and servants cried them out as the search for witches spread.

March 24 found elderly Rebecca Nurse standing before the judges. Though well loved for her good deeds by many in the village, still she had her enemies. At her examination the girls performed their latest trick. When Rebecca Nurse bent her head in thought, the girls bent their heads also. When she bit her lip or shifted her hands, the girls seemed forced to do the same. Any motion made by the poor woman was imitated by the bewitched girls, who wailed that she tortured them with bites and pinches.

Bravely the accused woman withstood Judge Hathorne's angry questions.

"I never afflicted no child never in my life," she insisted. "Would you have me belie myself?"

The judge ordered her clapped in leg irons and locked in Salem jail despite her claims of innocence.

Other suspected witches shared none of Rebecca Nurse's strength of character. In the hope of saving themselves from punishment, dozens of accused people confessed to things they never had done. Deliverance Hobbs admitted attending a witches' meeting in the pasture beside Mr. Parris's house. She swore she saw Osborne, Good, and Nurse there and that the devil, a tall black man in a high-crowned hat, threatened to tear her to pieces if she refused to sign his book. Ann Foster revealed that she rode on a pole with the devil and Martha Carrier "in the aire above the tops of the trees." They flew to the witches' Sabbath in Salem Village, she said, and drank wine as red as blood. She swore that as many as 305 witches existed in the colony.

Armed with such confessions and stung by the constant shrieks of the teenage girls, officers of the law continued the arrests. Martha Carrier soon was forced into chains, along with three of her children.

Against their wills, Sarah Cloyce and Mary Easty joined their stouthearted sister, Rebecca Nurse, in Salem jail.

Some of the bewitched girls clearly enjoyed their growing fame. The day before Goodwife Elizabeth Proctor's examination, a few of them sat laughing at the local inn. "There, Goody Proctor, there, Goody Proctor," they cried out, pointing to the rafters. "Old witch, I'll have her hang." Seeing they made a game of it all, the innkeeper sharply told them they lied. The children shrugged and giggled, one of them saying that "they must have some sport."

The girls now possessed complete power over the community. The few people who voiced doubts about the girls soon found themselves accused. On May 24 Nathaniel Cary of Charlestown brought his wife to Salem Village after hearing she was accused. At Ingersoll's inn they waited until all the girls came in and "tumbled down like swine." They cried out that his wife hurt them, and she was soon brought before the justices.

To get a confession the judges forced her "to stand with her arms stretched out," her husband later recalled. "I did request that I might hold one of her hands, but it was denied me; then she desired me to wipe the tears from her eyes and the sweat from her face, which I did; then she desired she should lean herself on me, saying she should faint." Judge Hathorne replied that she possessed strength enough to torment the girls, so she should have strength enough to stand.

When Boston sea captain John Alden arrived in Salem Village on May 31, he too was accused. He described that in the meetinghouse he saw "those wenches . . . play their juggling tricks, falling down, crying out, and staring in people's faces." One girl "had a man standing at her back to hold her up. He stooped down to her ear; then she cried out, Alden, Alden afflicted her." Down in the street a crowd surrounded him. The same tortured girl screamed, "There stands Alden. . . . He sells powder and shot to the Indians!" After that nothing could prevent his being carted off to jail.

Old women, husbands, wives, and strangers fell victim to the mounting frenzy. By the end of May the number charged with witchcraft crimes reached a shocking total of sixty-seven. From Maine to Connecticut the panic spread with a fear so real that in little Gloucester, Massachusetts, the frightened citizens actually shut themselves up in their stockade fort in an attempt to keep the devil out.

Alarmed by the crowded Salem and Boston jails, the colony's new royal governor, Sir William Phips, appointed a special court of seven judges. Headed by Lieutenant Governor William Stoughton, the judges met in the town of Salem to hear and determine the first of the witchcraft cases.

On June 2, the trial of Goodwife Bridget Bishop began. Many Salem villagers disliked Goody Bishop because of her unusual life-style. Against Puritan teachings she wore red clothing, often had fistfights with her husband, and owned a tavern where men drank and played a game similar to shuffleboard.

Suspected by some of witchcraft since 1680, when a neighborhood child mysteriously fell sick, the court now heard several kinds of evidence against her.

Past enemies of Goody Bishop remembered that scary things happened after arguments with her. William Stacy testified that he had passed Bishop on the road after a dispute. Suddenly the wheels of his horse cart "sunk down into a hole" that was not there before. Another time when he had tried to pass her his horse stood still so abruptly that "all his gears and tacking blew in pieces and the cart fell down." And one dark night while walking to his barn, Stacy claimed, he was somehow suddenly "hoisted from the ground and thrown against a stone wall." All these things he blamed on Bridget Bishop's curses.

Others swore that her spirit, or specter, tormented them. Richard Coman told the court that on a Saturday night Bishop's spirit had entered his room, "took hold of him by the throat and almost hauled him out of bed." Eighteen-year-old John Cook testified that one sunrise he had seen Bridget Bishop grinning in his bedchamber. Presently she "struck me on the side of the head which did very much hurt me." John Louder related that once in the dead of night he awakened to find "Bridget Bishop, or her likeness, sitting upon my stomach. . . . She presently . . . choked me and I had no strength or power in my hands to resist or help myself." Whether or not these men were relating dreams, the court willingly accepted this "specter" evidence.

It was believed that witches often used puppets to carry out their curses. By sticking pins in a doll, they inflicted injuries on the person it represented. John Bly and his son William revealed to the judges that they had found such puppets made of rags stuffed with hog bristles while tearing down the cellar wall in Bridget Bishop's old house.

Finally, nine women testified that they saw the devil's mark upon her body. Appointed by the court, they examined Goody Bishop and discovered an unusual mark or mole from which it was believed the devil could feed and draw strength. All of this "evidence," together with the screams and seizures of the always present teenage girls, persuaded the twelve-man jury. Despite Bridget Bishop's protests, they convicted her of witchcraft.

On June 10, 1692, hundreds of settlers climbed barren Gallows Hill to watch Bishop's sentence carried out. Sheriff Corwin reported that he brought

Goody Bishop out of Salem jail. He "Safely Conveyed her to the place provided for her Execution and Caused the said Brigett to be hanged by the neck until Shee was dead." The people of Salem had killed their first witch.

Upset by the severe attitude of the court, Judge Nathaniel Saltonstall resigned his seat. The trials continued nevertheless. At the start of every noisy courtroom session, the Reverend Mr. Noyes opened with a prayer. During each trial Judge Hathorne assisted with the questioning. Throughout the summer months court officials dragged in one suspected witch after another. In bewilderment they defended themselves, while the judges bullied them and the troubled children disrupted the hearings with new signs of their tortures.

During the June 30 trials of Sarah Good, Susannah Martin, Elizabeth Howe, Sarah Wilds, and Rebecca Nurse, thirty-seven friends of Rebecca Nurse presented a petition in her favor. It pleaded "we never had any cause or grounds to suspect her of any such thing as she is now accused of." In her case the jurymen first brought back a verdict of not guilty. Angrily Judge Stoughton forced them to reconsider. Finally Rebecca Nurse received the sentence of the others. On July 19 an aroused mob watched all five swing by ropes on Gallows Hill, but not before Sarah Good had laid her bloody curse on Mr. Noyes.

The court tried the case of eighty-year-old George Jacobs on August 5. Accused of being a male witch, or wizard, the white-haired man, who walked with two canes, remained defiant. "You tax me for a wizard," he cried. "You may as well tax me for a buzzard. I have done no harm." As the girls in the courtroom fell into "grievous fits and screechings," Jacobs looked around and shouted, "Well burn me or

hang me. . . . I know nothing of it." In the end the jury found him guilty after his own granddaughter testified against him. Later when she asked his forgiveness, he freely gave it to her.

Before noon on August 19, George Jacobs joined John Willard, John Proctor, Martha Carrier, and George Burroughs on the gallows ladders. Many people believed, in fact, that Carrier and Burroughs were the leaders of the witches. Burroughs, once the minister of Salem Village and now so close to death,

gave a final speech. He claimed his innocence and ended by reciting the Lord's Prayer perfectly, something a witch supposedly could never do. Poor John Willard tried five times to repeat the prayer as a test in court and failed.

From the scaffold Burroughs's words moved the crowd to tears and hesitation. Was it possible he spoke the truth? they wondered. In another moment the Reverend Cotton Mather pushed forward through the throng on horseback. The court had already handed down its verdict, he insisted. Finally persuaded, the crowd allowed the five executions to proceed. Afterwards, cut down and dragged to a shallow grave between the rocks nearby, Burroughs was buried with one of his hands and his chin left uncovered. People wanted a chance to touch the body of a witch for good luck.

The trials reached their peak in September. By then the witch-hunt had affected the lives of some 160 people chained in jail or executed. Elizabeth Proctor avoided following her husband to the gallows by "pleading her belly." The court pardoned the pregnant woman until after the birth of her baby. Nathaniel Cary's wife escaped from jail with the help of friends and ran away to safety in New York. John Alden escaped as well, hiding in the town of Duxbury.

Other prisoners were not so lucky. On September 22 eight more people, including Mary Easty and Martha Corey, were hanged on Gallows Hill. Afterwards the Reverend Mr. Noyes calmly observed, "What a sad thing it is to see eight firebrands of Hell hanging there."

Two days earlier, Martha Corey's husband suffered the strangest and most painful punishment of all. Accused in court of witchcraft, crusty old

Giles Corey refused to plead either guilty or not
guilty. Because the court seized the property of
guilty men, he bravely believed he could save his
farm for his sons by standing silent. To force a confession, the judges sentenced Corey to be stretched
out in an open field. Heavy stones were placed on his
chest until he either confessed or was crushed to
death. Later children sang a song about his fate.

Giles Corey he said not a word,
No single word spoke he.
"Giles Corey," saith the magistrate,
"We'll press it out of thee."
They got them then a heavy beam,
They laid it on his breast,
They loaded it with heavy stones,
And hard upon him pressed.
"More weight!" now said this wretched man;
"More weight!" again he cried;
And he did no confession make,
But wickedly he died.

The widespread killings of September shocked many in the community. On October 3 Cotton Mather's father, the Reverend Increase Mather, stated, "It were better that ten suspected witches should escape than that one innocent person should be condemned." As the hysterical girls accused more important and respected citizens, doubts arose about their truthfulness. Finally when Governor Phips heard his own wife's name mentioned as a witch, he decided the court "must fall." He sent the judges home and passed a law that stopped the use of specter evidence in witchcraft trials. In the following months the panic lessened and people slowly returned to their senses. The Salem witchcraft terror left in its wake Giles Corey pressed to death, nineteen men and women hanged, and others, like Sarah Osborne, dead from sickness in jail.

In time many of those possessed by fear realized the tragedy they had caused. In 1697 the members of the witchcraft jury publicly asked forgiveness, declaring "we were sadly deluded and mistaken." Judge Samuel Sewall joined them in admitting he was wrong. In 1706 one of the hysterical girls, Anne Putnam, now a woman, repented her part in the panic. In church she proclaimed, "I desire to lie in the dust . . . in that I was a cause of so much calamity." By 1711, when the governor awarded money to the families of those condemned in the trials, the controversy seemed at an end.

Today Salem Village is part of Danvers, Massachusetts, and Rebecca Nurse's grave can still be seen in the family burial plot. One modern scientist has suggested that the Salem girls ate bread made from wheat infected with a fungus that caused their fits and visions. Though most people do not believe in witches anymore, there are still a few who point out the frightening power of Sarah Good's curse. "If you take away my life God will give you blood to drink!" she had threatened the Reverend Mr. Noyes. People in Salem noted that, twenty-five years later, when a blood vessel burst in the minister's head, he died choking on his own blood.

About the Author

Zachary Kent grew up in the town of Little Falls, New Jersey. He is a graduate of St. Lawrence University and holds a teaching certificate in English. Following college he was employed at a New York City literary agency for two years until he decided to launch a career as a writer. To support himself while writing, he has worked as a taxi driver, a shipping clerk, and a house painter.

Mr. Kent has had a lifelong interest in American history. As a boy the study of the United States presidents was his special hobby. His collection of presidential items includes books, pictures, and games, as well as several autographed letters.

About the Artist

Ralph Canaday has been involved in all aspects of commercial art since graduation from the Art Institute of Chicago in 1959. He is an illustrator, designer, painter, and sculptor whose work has appeared in many national publications, textbooks, and corporate promotional materials. Mr. Canaday lives in Hanover Park, Illinois, with his wife Arlene, who is also in publishing.